ALISON PEARCE STEVENS

ILLUSTRATED BY JASON FORD

GODWINBOOKS

Henry Holt and Company
New York

Henry Holt and Company, *Publishers since 1866*
Henry Holt® is a registered trademark of Macmillan Publishing Group, LLC
120 Broadway, New York, NY 10271 • mackids.com

Our books may be purchased in bulk for promotional, educational, or business use. Please
contact your local bookseller or the Macmillan Corporate and Premium Sales Department at
(800) 221-7945 ext. 5442 or by email at MacmillanSpecialMarkets@macmillan.com.

Library of Congress Control Number: 2023028891

First edition, 2024
Book design by Jen Keenan
Printed in China by RR Donnelley Asia Printing Solutions Ltd., Dongguan City, Guangdong
Province

ISBN 978-1-250-84734-8
10 9 8 7 6 5 4 3 2 1

FOR JEFF, COLE, AND LANE:
THANKS FOR WORKING WITH ME
TO BE CLIMATE HEROES

MEET THE
SUPERVILLAIN

Wildfires raging across Canada and Greece. Flooding in the western United States. A heat wave launching temperatures to 100° Fahrenheit (38° Celsius) in Siberia. Permafrost melting, turning solid ground into a mushy mess. Tropical storms forming, one after the other, pummeling cities on land again and again. A massive storm called a *derecho* flattening crops and buildings across the middle of the country.

And that was just 2023.

Whoa—are we under attack? What supervillain could possibly be causing so much damage?

Meet climate change. It's not a living, breathing super-villain, but it acts like one just the same. Every year, the effects of climate change get worse. Record-setting natural disasters happen more often. More land burns. More rain falls—or none at all. Temperatures soar to new heights. Stronger storms kick up more damaging winds.

Sounds like it's time to call in some superheroes! What heroes, you ask? You. Me. Anyone who cares about the planet we live on. Our voices and our actions are our superpowers. We can change the world when we try.

We also need to call on a special group of heroes. They're already out there in the wild, working to keep our climate in check, and we need their help. Who are these climate heroes?

GREAT WHALES—Fighting climate change with massive "poo-nados"!

SEA OTTERS—Fuzzy cuteness keeping kelp in its place!

FOREST ELEPHANTS— Strengthening forests by trampling trees!

ECHIDNAS—Burying climate change with mighty claws!

We need these heroes to amp up their activities to help us win this fight.

Where did climate change come from? Scientists around the world agree: It was created by people. Not on purpose! But just about everything we do releases carbon into the air. Even though climate change is our nemesis, carbon is really at work here. It's like the puppet master, pulling the strings, causing the planet to warm. If we want to tackle climate change, we have to zero in on carbon.

WHAT'S CARBON'S DEAL ANYWAY?

Carbon is one of the 118 elements scientists have identified. But it isn't just any old element. It's the stuff of coal—and diamond. We burn it for heat and electricity. And it's in every bite of food we eat. Carbon is the building block of all living things, including you.

Why carbon? It plays nice with other elements. It likes to form chemical bonds and it's not picky about which elements it joins. That versatility allows it to make up the backbone of all kinds of living (and nonliving) things.

Carbon is also in Earth's crust, its oceans, and its atmosphere. That last one is where it's causing problems. Carbon is the heart of two greenhouse gases: carbon dioxide (CO_2) and methane (CH_4). When these gases enter our atmosphere, they trap the sun's heat close to Earth. It's

Heat causes water molecules to evaporate from the ocean's surface. They gather in the air to form clouds.

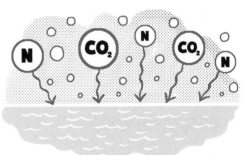

Nitrogen (N) and carbon dioxide (CO_2) move in the other direction, absorbed from the air by water.

kind of like how a blanket traps your body heat, keeping you warm at night. Or how glass on a car or greenhouse traps heat inside on a sunny day.

Greenhouse gases (Get it? They trap heat like a *greenhouse*?) are a good thing—to a certain extent. Without them, Earth would be a ball of ice. It's thanks to these greenhouse gases that we not only have liquid water, but have life on this planet at all.

But too much of a good thing is NEVER good. People's actions have been adding more and more greenhouse gases to our atmosphere. It's like piling on the blankets until you're just . . . too . . . HOT! In the same way, our planet is getting too warm. And that spells trouble for everything, from the tiniest ocean dwellers to the tallest plants to every person on the planet and everything in between.

One solution is to find ways to lock that carbon away. Whether it's deep in the ocean, underground, or in forests on land, taking carbon out of the atmosphere can help us get climate change under control. That's where our climate heroes come in.

UNSUNG HEROES

Before we get to our first animal hero, we should take a peek at the unsung heroes of climate change. These heroes aren't the kind of organisms you think about much—if at

all. Yet they're always there in the background, sucking carbon out of the atmosphere and turning it into something new. As you will see, our superheroes work with these unsung heroes to fight climate change.

Who are these mysterious climate heroes? Plants, algae, and cyanobacteria. If you were to take a stroll to a pond or lake to observe them, they wouldn't seem to do much. But these heroes share a climate-changing superpower: photosynthesis. Without them, carbon would stay in the atmosphere, warming the planet and wreaking havoc. Their photosynthesis is the first step in a chain reaction to stop climate change.

Here's how it works:

Algae and plants use photosynthesis to make their own food. Plants need food, too! But algae and plants are incredible because *they make their own food*. As if that's not enough? They make food *from air*.

Plants use carbon dioxide and water to make sugar with help from sunlight. They don't need the leftover oxygen, so they release it into the air (lucky for us—we need it to breathe!).

Photosynthesis creates sugar. To be clear, this isn't like the sugary cereal you might eat for breakfast—though that sugar also came from plants, probably sugar cane or sugar beets. Sugar is the base of all carbohydrates, including starch and fiber. And it all comes from plants. Photosynthesis is a kind of magic, er . . . science, called chemistry. And it provides food for (almost) every living thing on the planet.

But that's not all! Photosynthesis doesn't just turn carbon dioxide into sugar. The process also kicks out extra oxygen—the very thing we need to breathe. (Fun fact: Trees get a lot of credit for releasing oxygen, but more than *half* of the oxygen you breathe comes from the ocean.) Trees provide food and shelter for animals of all kinds, including people. They shade us on hot days and protect us from strong winds. We use their lumber to build homes and furniture.

Organisms of all kinds do "jobs" that benefit us. It's easy to overlook those ecosystem services. But they are vitally important for us—and all life on Earth.

FIGHTING CLIMATE CHANGE WITH **MASSIVE POO-NADOS!**

What weighs more than 10 tons (10.2 metric tons), has collapsible lungs, and breathes through the top of its head? The biggest climate hero on the planet, that's who!

Let's meet the first of our animal heroes out on the open ocean. We're a *l-o-n-g* way from land. There's nothing but water as far as the eye can see. The surface bobs in gentle swells. It reflects sunlight, making you squint. And the water is so deep, you can't see anything as you try to peer into its depths.

It looks like there's a clear line between water and air. But if you put your super-shrinking abilities to good use,

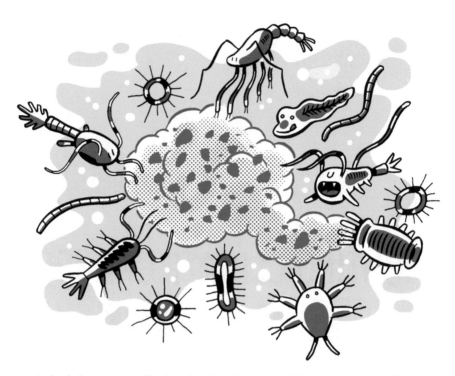

Let's shrink down even smaller than these itty-bitty critters called zooplankton. We'll see them again soon.

you'll see them interact. Let's get super small—a tiny fraction of the period at the end of this sentence—so we can see what's going on.

After being warmed by the sun, some water molecules leave the ocean and become water vapor. The warmer it is, the more water molecules evaporate. They rise high into the atmosphere where they form clouds. Those clouds may gather into a massive storm that travels hundreds or thousands of miles, dumping water on land far, far away. (This is how warming causes bigger storms.)

Molecules of nitrogen and carbon dioxide, on the other

hand, mainly move in the other direction. They dissolve into the ocean's waters. It's thanks to our oceans that climate change didn't happen faster. Our planet's vast waters have absorbed a HUGE amount of the carbon dioxide we've pumped out.

What happens to that carbon has a big impact on climate. If it sinks into the ocean's depths, it will get locked away for hundreds, maybe thousands of years. That's like yanking off the blankets and stuffing them deep in a closet and forgetting they're there. But if carbon stays close to the surface, it can return to the atmosphere and cause more warming.

That movement of carbon is the key to our first heroes' planet-saving actions. They help remove carbon from the atmosphere and drive it into the bottom of the ocean.

Speaking of which, where are our heroes? They're deep below us, where sunlight dims to near darkness. Grunts and groans fill the water as they keep in touch by sound. They power through clouds of shrimplike krill hiding from predators in the dark depths. But our heroes find them. They gulp them down by the thousands. Then they shoot the water out through their comblike baleen before swallowing the leftover lumps of their favorite seafood.

Who are these heroes? Great whales. When they surface, they will unleash their superpower—a massive poo-nado of goopy poop.

MEET THE CLIMATE HEROES: GREAT WHALES

The biggest climate heroes are some of the biggest animals on Earth. Meet the great whales that help keep our oceans going strong.

Most great whales are baleen whales. Instead of teeth, they have long, fringed sheets of baleen used to catch krill and other small critters. They take in a mouthful, then use their tongues to push the water out, trapping their wriggling prey against the baleen. The bigger the whale, the more it eats. The more it eats, the bigger its poo-nado. But that's not all. The more it eats, the more carbon it stores inside its body.

BLUE WHALE—Weighing in at a whopping 380,000 pounds (172 metric tons), blue whales are thought to be the largest animals to *ever* roam the planet. (Imagine putting 29 of the biggest elephants you've ever seen together—that's how much one blue whale weighs.) The biggest whales are more than 100 feet (30 meters) from tip to tail, about two and a half school buses long. A single blue whale contains 22,800 pounds (10.3 metric tons) of carbon—that's as much as five minivans weigh!

BOWHEAD WHALE—These whales live in the icy waters of the Arctic, using their thick skulls to smash through giant sheets of ice. They have the longest baleen plates of any whales, using them to feed on krill, copepods, and other small critters, including small fish. They may live to be 200 years old!

FIN WHALE—Named for the hooked fin on the back, fin whales love the open ocean. Sleek and streamlined, these fast swimmers torpedo through the water in search of food. They fill their expandable throats with water, then filter out each meal through hundreds of baleen plates.

RIGHT WHALE—Found in both northern and southern seas, usually close to shore, these whales are slow swimmers. Their smooth, black bodies become white and bumpy along the head and jaw. The patches are often home to parasites called whale lice.

HUMPBACK WHALE—With their hunched backs, knobby heads, and long flippers, humpbacks are expert hunters. They trap prey by blowing spiraling circles of bubbles around schools of their favorite fish. Then they power into the bubble net, sometimes using their flippers to guide prey into their mouths.

GRAY WHALE—Naturally curious, gray whales are likely to check out whale-watching boats and the people on them. They plow through the seafloor in search of food, swimming on their sides while they suck up mud and hidden critters from the sandy bottom.

SEI WHALE—Pronounced "say" whale, these whales are fast swimmers, topping out faster than 34 miles per hour (55 kilometers per hour). Unlike most whales, they don't lift their tails out of the water before diving. But they do leave "fluke prints" on the surface of the water—smooth circles left behind by underwater movement of the tail flukes.

BRYDE'S WHALE—Pronounced "broodus" whale, these whales are similar to sei whales but prefer warmer water. They spend most of their time near the surface but dive as deep as 1,000 feet (305 meters) in search of fish, krill, and copepods. They sometimes use bubble nets to feed.

MINKE WHALE—The smallest of the great whales, these sleek animals sneak up on plankton and fish by lunging at them from the side. In areas with ice, they often "spyhop" by poking their heads above the surface. Their curious nature brings them close to boats.

SPERM WHALE—These are the only great whales without baleen. They have teeth that they use to hunt giant squid *d-e-e-p* in the ocean. (They can dive more than 3,900 feet, or 1.2 kilometers, almost three-quarters of a mile!) There's no light down there, so they use loud clicks to find their prey, just like bats searching for insects.

We're still out on the open ocean. The gentle swells on the surface start to shimmer. They roil and bubble. Our heroes are barreling toward the light from the ocean depths, because they aren't fish. They need to breathe air just like we do. After feeding, whales swim to the surface. One breaks through, shooting a spray of water, air, and snot out of its nostril-like blowhole before sucking in a new breath. And it poops—a massive, whale-sized cloud of woolly waste streams out behind it. The poo-nado usually doesn't sink. It floats on the water, slowly spreading out. And even though most people would probably swim away as fast as they could, tiny critters called copepods flock to it. These itty-bitty relatives of shrimp and lobsters chow down on the nutritious goop.

That's not all. The poo-nado is like compost dumped on a garden. All that waste is chock-full of nutrients. It's not just the copepods and other zooplankton that eat it up. Whale poop is full of nitrogen, phosphorous, and iron. Next time your parent or guardian drags you to a home improvement store, take a look at a bag of fertilizer—it lists how much nitrogen and phosphorous is inside. Those are nutrients that plants need to grow. Not just plants—all living things that photosynthesize, including phytoplankton.

Those nutrients are often in limited supply. So if you increase how much is available, plants and algae can grow faster. They take carbon dioxide from the air and use it to make food and new cells. They get bigger. For the single-celled algae that make up phytoplankton,

POO-NADO

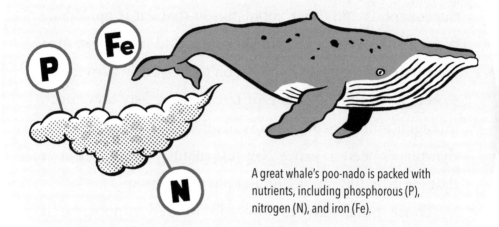

A great whale's poo-nado is packed with nutrients, including phosphorous (P), nitrogen (N), and iron (Fe).

fertilizer means they divide more often, each cell splitting in two, over and over and over again. Our unsung heroes are hard at work, sucking up carbon dioxide as they grow. Soon we get an algal bloom. The top layer of the ocean has so many phytoplankton, they can be seen from space!

The whale just added a massive dose of fertilizer to the ocean's surface. And since this whale has a baby, it's not alone. The youngster breaches the surface, taking in fresh air and leaving its own poo-nado in its wake. In the distance, you see another whale spout. There might be a poo-nado here, too. (They don't poop every time they come up for air, so we don't know for sure.) With every massive poop, the surface of the ocean gets fertilized a bit more.

It won't be long before an algal bloom develops. Those phytoplankton will feed zooplankton, which will feed small fish, which will feed large fish, and so on. Sunlight provides the energy and poo-nados provide the nutrients. Phytoplankton take those essential ingredients and churn out a buffet that supports life throughout the ocean.

That's super important—but not the end of our carbon story. Every time an animal eats, its body takes a bunch of the carbon in that food and turns it into parts of its *own* body. As they say: You are what you eat! Unlike you, fish never stop growing. Once you reach a certain size, growth plates in your bones will harden, stopping your growth. Fish don't have that issue. They just keep increasing in size. When big fish die, they sink deep down to the bottom of the ocean, where their bodies become food for the animals living in the dark depths. The bigger the fish, the more carbon is carried to the seafloor.

The same thing happens with whales. They're not fish, and each species does seem to reach a maximum size, but the bigger the whale, the more carbon its body contains. When a whale dies, the resulting whale fall creates a feast. Bottom-dwelling animals come from far and wide to chow down. The carbon from the whale becomes carbon in those animals' bodies. And when they die, that carbon either dissolves into deep ocean water or gets buried in the sediment on the seafloor.

Although carbon dioxide moves between air and water at the ocean's surface, water at the bottom is too far away for those gases to make the trip back up to the atmosphere. The carbon is locked away for hundreds, even thousands of years.

Great whales are climate heroes in life because their poo-nados fertilize the oceans. They're heroes again when they die and sink to the seafloor, taking their carbon with them.

MEET THE PLANKTON!

The ocean may look like it's just a bunch of water, but it's actually teeming with life. And not only a whale here or a fish there. Billions upon billions of critters drift through our planet's waters. Either too small or too weak to fight against a current, these drifters are called plankton. They're the base of the ocean's food web. No plankton? No fish. No whales. Hardly any life at all.

Most of our whale heroes eat fish and zooplankton. They especially like those copepods. (Try not to think too much about whales eating the critters that ate their poop!) Even better, they like krill. These small, shrimplike animals live in massive groups in the open ocean. They're a popular food for lots of animals, so krill and other types of zooplankton swim down, down into the dark during the day, where they're harder to spot. At night, they swim back up to the surface to feed on smaller plankton.

Other zooplankton include larvae from animals that will eventually get much bigger. Fish larvae, for example. Or the larvae from sea urchins, clams, and other animals that will live on the ocean floor. Jellyfish are also zooplankton. Even though this group includes some of the longest animals in the sea (some are longer than a blue whale!), they're weak swimmers. If they can't fight the current, they're considered plankton.

But not all plankton is made up of animals. Some of it is phytoplankton. These include algae and bacteria that use photosynthesis just like plants do. Phytoplankton are super tiny, but they are THE base of the ocean food web. Almost all energy in the ocean starts with them. And they're the key to our heroes' climate-fighting actions. Think of them as the super-secret, practically invisible sidekick.

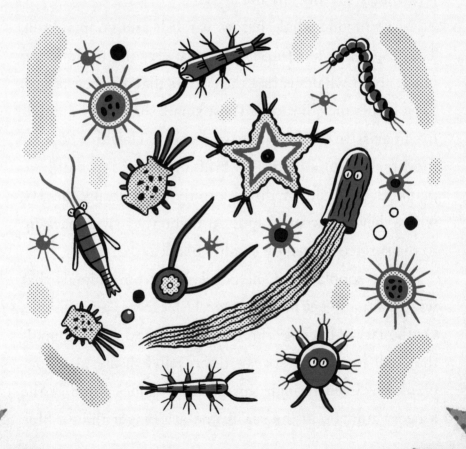

HELPING OUR HEROES

It's not just ocean animals that rely on those phytoplankton and the fish they feed. The more fish we have, the more food there is for everyone—including people. Whales with their poo-nados turn out to be a key player in keeping those fisheries alive. Unfortunately for whales, people didn't understand that link until recently.

People used to hunt whales for oil, meat, and blubber. Some Indigenous people still do—it's an important part of their way of life. A single whale can support a band of people for a long time, so they don't hunt very many whales. It's the few countries that still allow whale hunting on a big scale that make it an issue. Those whale hunts kill many more of these majestic animals. It's been happening for more than a thousand years—long enough to vastly reduce the number of whales in our oceans.

More recently, people argued that we needed to remove whales to protect fisheries. They thought whales ate too many fish, and if they removed the whales then there would be more food for people. But hunting whales actually had the opposite effect. Without whales, there weren't poo-nados bringing nutrients up from the depths. That meant less phytoplankton, less zooplankton, and fewer fish to go around.

Today, people are fighting to protect whales. Before you were born, thousands of whales were killed each year. Now it's just a few hundred, and groups of people are working to bring that number closer to zero. They're working to convince countries that allow whale hunting to shift to ecotourism. People will pay money to see a whale in the wild. The hotels where they stay and the restaurants they visit during their trip also make money. Whale-watching ecotourism can replace the money those countries made from hunting while leaving our climate heroes alive and well.

But even without hunting, whales still face serious problems. They can be killed by ships or by getting tangled in fishing lines and nets. People are working to fix those problems, too.

What can YOU do to help whales? See if your parents will take you on a whale-watching tour on your next family vacation. Or if you live close to the ocean, participate in a beach cleanup. Not an option? You can make changes right at home that can help protect the ocean. One of the biggest? Use less plastic.

A huge amount of the plastic we use makes its way to the ocean—even if we use that plastic thousands of miles away from the shoreline. That's because plastic breaks down into ever-smaller pieces that get blown by wind and washed by rain. Those bits and pieces tumble into streams and rivers and eventually get washed into the sea where animals—including whales—get tangled in them or mistake them for food.

To help whales and other marine animals, avoid using single-use plastics, like plastic bags, straws, or plastic wrap. Replace them with a cloth bag, metal or paper straws, and a reusable container. Also avoid buying bottled water. Those bottles often wind up in the ocean. Instead, find a good, reusable water bottle and fill it with filtered tap water.

Also talk to your adults about buying local. It's easy to order items online, but they are often shipped to us from the other side of the world. Those container ships pose a major threat to whales. Keeping your purchases closer to home goes a long way to protecting our climate heroes.

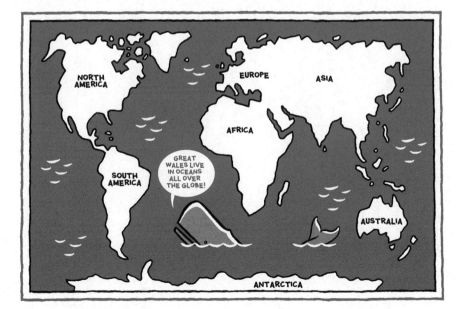

FUZZY CUTENESS
KEEPING KELP IN ITS PLACE!

What can hold its breath for five minutes, has the densest fur of any mammal, and uses armpit pockets to fight climate change? Meet our next climate hero!

We've moved closer to land now, just off the coast of California. Here those bobbing deep-ocean swells build into towering waves that curl and crash against the rocky coastline. You squint against the sea spray as you look for our next hero. Gulls wheel through the air. Sea lions bark from a rocky outcrop. It smells like salt water, fish, and stinky sea lion and bird poop—no shortage of nutrients

here. Pee-yew! Maybe we should move upwind a bit.

The surface of the water here isn't smooth, and not just because of the waves. In the trough between each incoming swell the water looks rough and bumpy. Here and there it's dotted with larger lumps. Let's dive beneath the surface to see what's going on.

As soon as you drop down into the water, you're surrounded. Flat, leaflike blades slap against you as an incoming wave pushes them in your direction. You swim away only to run into more blades. These aren't sharp, cutting blades. They can't hurt you. But you could get tangled up. These blades are the leaflike parts of kelp. You've dropped right into a kelp forest. That's right: an underwater forest! This forest is our unsung hero in this ecosystem. More on that later.

The kelp grows from the rocky bottom all the way to the top of the water. Kelp isn't strong enough to poke out into the air, so when it reaches the surface, it fans out, forming a canopy. All that kelp is what makes the water look so rough from up above.

The kelp wiggles as the water flows by, wafting toward land with incoming waves, then back again as the current flows out to sea. It's peaceful here, calm. The kelp slows the movement of waves, stopping them from pounding against you. Fish swim by. Snails creep along. A shadow looms over you, and you glance up, nervous. Is it a shark?

The shadow darts toward you and pauses. If you could breathe down here, you'd let out a big sigh of relief. It's not a shark, it's our next hero! A curious sea otter inspects you before diving down into the depths. A minute later

THE SEA OTTER!

CAN HOLD BREATH FOR UP TO FIVE MINUTES

VERY DENSE FUR

POWERFUL JAWS AND TEETH

ARMPIT POCKETS

WEBBED HIND FEET

it shoots back up toward the surface, wriggling its body and pushing against the water with its webbed hind feet. Purple spikes poke out from its front paws. It's clutching a sea urchin.

You follow it up to the surface. (Time to take a breath!) The otter rolls onto its back, knocks the spines off the urchin with a powerful swipe of its paw, and wedges the round body between its teeth. The urchin's hard, round test (internal skeleton) cracks in two, and the otter chows down on the insides, drops the remains in the water, then pulls another urchin from under its armpit. Time for a second course!

MEET THE CLIMATE HEROES:
SEA OTTERS

Unlike whales, sea otters aren't big—in fact, they're the smallest of all marine mammals. But their role in this ecosystem is *mighty*! They protect our unsung kelp heroes from grazers. The otters' secret weapons? Strong teeth and powerful jaws. Webbed hind feet that they use to propel themselves through the water. And armpit pockets where they stash food while hunting.

The biggest sea otters stretch up to 5 feet (1.5 meters) long and weigh in at 100 pounds (45 kilograms). Sea otters ring the northern Pacific Ocean, living along coastlines from Japan to California. No matter where sea otters live, these heroes not only keep the ecosystems running strong, they also help fight climate change by protecting kelp forests from sea urchins and other grazing animals.

Sea otters live their entire lives in cold water. They keep warm with the densest fur of any animal. It's so thick, water never touches a sea otter's skin! Their broad, rounded teeth can crack open the shells of urchins, snails, clams, mussels, and crabs. They use those teeth—a lot! Because they live in cold water, sea otters burn lots of energy keeping their internal temperature nice and toasty.

A single otter uses its powerful bite to swallow the soft insides of 15 to 18 pounds (7 to 8 kilograms) of hard-shelled animals per day: crabs, sea urchins, snails, clams, mussels, and abalone. Climate hero extraordinaire! (Not

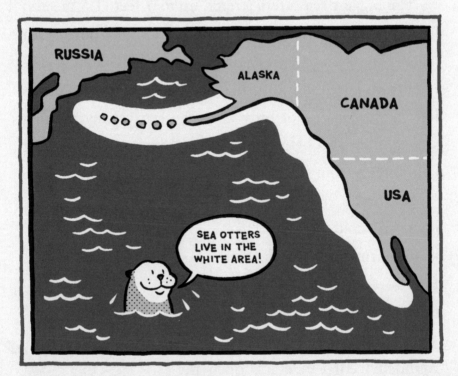

Otter distribution in the upper Pacific Ocean.

all sea otters like urchins, but it's easy to spot the ones that do—their teeth turn bright purple.)

What does a spiky purple dinner have to do with climate change? More than you might think. Remember that algae use photosynthesis to remove carbon from the atmosphere. That was true of tiny phytoplankton, and it's true of massive algae, too—like kelp. The bigger the kelp, the more carbon it can store in its own tissues, and the better it is for our climate.

When kelp dies, some of it sinks to the seafloor. From there, it may slide off the continental shelf, down, *down*, *d-o-w-n* into the depths of the open ocean. Once it goes deep enough, the carbon it contains can't return to the surface—not for centuries. That's what makes kelp our unsung climate hero.

But that only happens if kelp sinks to the ocean floor. When kelp breaks free from the rocky bottom, it floats. Some may drift out into the ocean and sink, but the rest will wash up on shore or simply decay in shallow water. When this happens, it delivers important nutrients to the land. But the carbon stored in its tissues returns to the atmosphere as carbon dioxide. Keeping kelp anchored—and growing—is critical for fighting climate change.

The bad news? It's anchored in place! That's great for kelp forests and all the animals that live there. After all, you wouldn't want your home to wash away in a storm. But it's not so great when kelp eaters get out of control. Kelp can't go anywhere if it's under attack. And if something happens to our sea otter heroes, purple sea urchins launch a full-scale assault against the forest.

You're about to see just how villainous purple urchins can be. But—and this is *important*—sea urchins are an essential part of marine ecosystems. They live in coastal waters, munching on kelp and  algae. You can think of them as the cleanup crew, vacuuming up the stuff that falls on the floor. Even though they can be a problem for kelp forests, they aren't truly villains. They keep algae in check. The ecosystem needs them—in small doses.

When there are too many urchins, the cleanup crew turns into an army. And armies require a *whole lot* of food. That's when sea urchins become a problem. Hordes of urchins stream across the rocky floor, eating any algae and kelp in their path. When there aren't loose pieces on the seafloor, the urchins climb up the kelp to munch on the blades. Sometimes they don't bother climbing that far, they just grind away at the stalk with their powerful jaws and teeth.

That's REALLY bad news for our unsung heroes. Urchins can chew right through the thick stalk, breaking the kelp free from its anchor. When there are too many urchins, they mow down every last stalk. Not only is kelp no longer storing carbon, much of it is tossed onto the beaches, where the carbon can return to the atmosphere. Having too many urchins is like tossing another blanket on the bed. But sea otters and other predators, like sea stars, keep things in check.

When predators are around, urchins spend most of their time hiding. They crawl into crevices where they're tough to find. Without our climate heroes, urchins are out and about all the time. Since they eat so much, they have lots of energy to reproduce, which means more and more urchins and less and less kelp.

Over time (but not very much time—just a few months), purple urchins can destroy entire kelp forests. Instead of a lush underwater forest, the rocky reef is covered in purple urchins searching in vain for something to eat.

Keeping sea otter populations healthy is essential for protecting kelp forests. The more otters we have, the more time urchins spend hiding. That means more kelp can grow (and grow it does!), storing more carbon in its tissues. That kelp stays anchored, so more of it sinks to the ocean depths when it dies, taking all that carbon with it.

MEET THE MINIVILLAIN
(BUT NOT REALLY):
PURPLE SEA URCHINS

A sea urchin looks like a little ball of spikes, but it's a living animal. The central body has test (remember, this is a hard skeleton), covered with a thin layer of tissue. (Imagine having your bones right under your skin—it's like that.) The test is tough for most animals to crack, but it's actually the urchin's third line of defense. The first? Movable spines jut out all over the urchin's body, making any predator think twice about trying to eat the animal inside. And if the urchin *is* attacked, tiny pincers rise up between the spines to snap at the attacker. A quick nip can be enough to make a hungry sea star find food somewhere else.

Do urchins walk on their spines? Nope. They use tube feet. Their bodies are covered in these long, delicate structures. The end of each one is shaped like a tiny suction cup so it can grab onto rock, algae, or the glass of an aquarium. Urchins extend their tube feet, stretching them out past the tips of their spines, so they can "walk" while staying protected from most predators. If you watch an urchin move, it seems to glide across the ground.

Urchins can't see where they're going, but they're good at finding algae and kelp. Their tube feet hold a secret of their own: They can detect odors in the water. That's right—urchins smell with their feet! They follow the scent until they find dinner.

And they are excellent eaters. Their secret weapon is a mouth ringed with five self-sharpening teeth. If a tooth is damaged, the urchin just grows a new one. Same with spines! These critters can cause maximum damage while staying safe from most predators.

Remember, though, that even though a horde of urchins can decimate a kelp forest, urchins are still an essential part of this ecosystem. They're only villainous in large numbers.

THE PURPLE SEA URCHIN!

SPINES

MOUTH WITH FIVE SHARP TEETH

PINCERS

TUBE FEET

MEET THE KELP!

Kelp is about as different from phytoplankton as you can get. They both photosynthesize, but phytoplankton are tiny and kelp can be HUGE! It also looks rather plantlike.

These organisms anchor themselves to underwater reefs. These reefs aren't made of coral. They're a string of rocky outcrops in the shallow-ish waters along the coast. Those rocks make the perfect spot for kelp, which grows a sprawling anchor that grips the rocky bottom. Although the anchor looks like a ball of roots, it doesn't work the way a plant's roots do. The anchor's job is to hold the kelp in place—that's it. Kelp doesn't absorb water or nutrients through roots. But it has to hold on tight, even during massive storms.

The main stalk grows straight up toward the light. Some species, like giant kelp, have blades growing along the whole length of that stalk. These blades each have a little balloon-like air bladder where they connect to the stalk. This keeps the kelp growing up toward the surface instead of falling on its side. Other species, like bull kelp, have a single air bladder at the top of the stalk. All of a bull kelp's blades grow from that bladder, sort of like a pom-pom.

Kelp grows in dense forests that are home to all kinds of hard-shelled animals, like snails, crabs, sea urchins, and sea stars. Young fish spend lots of time hiding among the blades. They're safe there, and there's plenty of food so they can grow big enough to avoid predators. And sea otters wrap themselves in the blades to nap—or use them as a babysitter when Mom needs to dive for food.

Giant kelp can grow up to 175 feet (53 meters) tall. It grows fastest in the spring, a whopping 2 feet (0.6 meters) per day. You can watch it grow right before your eyes! All that time, it's busy sucking up carbon dioxide and turning it into more kelp.

THE MIGHTY KELP!

GIANT KELP

BULL KELP

AIR BLADDER

ANCHOR

HELPING OUR HEROES

Keeping our coastal ecosystems going strong is essential for protecting our climate heroes. People who live in coastal states with sea otters are working hard to protect them. If you live in California, ask the adults in your life to donate to the California Sea Otter Fund when they do their taxes. When you visit anyplace along the Pacific with kelp forests and sea otters, be sure to view these heroes from a safe distance, so they're not disturbed by your presence. Stressed otters can become sick otters.

If you don't live near a sea otter habitat, you can still help! Call a family meeting—it's time to have a talk with your parents or guardians. They may not like what you have to say, so you might want to butter them up with a nice snack: some fresh fruit, perhaps, or almonds or sweet peppers. If all else fails, pull out the ice cream.

What are you going to talk about? Lawn care.

You may live a thousand miles from the coast, but how the adults in your life treat their yard still matters to the oceans—way more than you might think. Many Americans want a perfect green carpet outside their homes. But the only way to get that level of perfection is by using a whole lot of chemicals. Herbicides and pesticides kill off weeds and insects. Fertilizers help the grass grow.

It's easy to think those chemicals stay where we put them, but they don't. When we water the lawn or get a good rain, those chemicals run downhill. They keep moving until they reach streams and ponds. Ever seen a pond covered in scummy algae? That happens because of fertilizers from surrounding areas. Remember that fertilizer helps algae grow. But too much algae can be a real problem. It cuts off light to the plants below. When it dies, the bacteria that break it down use up all the oxygen, which kills off fish and other animals living in the water.

Many of our lawn chemicals travel all the way to the ocean. They dump pesticides and fertilizers into our coastal waters. Explosions of algae can happen near the mouth of a river. Not just big algae, like our kelp, but also the tiny phytoplankton.

Problem is, some kinds of phytoplankton release toxins. These toxins are what cause food poisoning when people eat contaminated seafood. Animals that eat them become sick or even die. And huge amounts of decaying algae can use up the oxygen from large areas of water. Fish and other animals can suffocate. Where the Mississippi River reaches the Gulf of Mexico, there's a huge dead zone where there's no life. That's due to chemical runoff from lawns and farms upriver.

But you can help! If your lawn has been fertilized regularly, it doesn't need more fertilizer. It's just going to wash away. Need another argument for your adults? It's a big waste of money. Overseeding with new grass seed each year can keep the lawn lush and thick without all those chemicals. Letting a few weeds grow is okay, too. Clover takes nitrogen from the air and fixes it in the ground, fertilizing the grass around it—for free! Lawns that have flowering plants, which many people consider weeds, are actually super important for pollinators (but they're the heroes of another story).

Instead of working so hard to fight nature—which sure wouldn't allow a perfect carpet of grass—it's a whole lot easier to work with it. Your yard will be healthier, YOU will be healthier. And the whole planet benefits, including our sea otter heroes.

STRENGTHENING FORESTS
BY **TRAMPLING TREES!**

What's 10 feet tall, super secretive, and tends the forest like a gardener? One of the rarest climate heroes of all.

We're moving up onto land and taking a big jump to the other side of the planet. Welcome to the tropical forests of central Africa. Before you, wide, wall-like buttress roots flare out from a towering tree. They stretch high above your head along the tree's trunk and sprawl in all directions across the forest floor. Unlike kelp's anchor, these roots are true roots. They hold the tree in place and slurp up water and nutrients from the soil. This tree—and other massive trees in this forest—are the unsung heroes here.

The air smells faintly of flowers. Fallen nuts and fruit crunch and squish beneath your feet as you make your way through the forest. Insects buzz, birds sing, and monkeys hoot. It's dark under the tall forest canopy. Little sunlight reaches the forest floor, so it's also fairly cool. Up ahead, light breaks through the trees. Let's go see what's over there.

As you get closer to the clearing, your feet snag on more and more undergrowth. Shrubby trees and vines compete for space, making it almost impossible to walk. Then they're gone. A well-trampled path appears in front of you, and it's headed right for the clearing. Cautiously— because who knows what kinds of critters use the path— you make your way toward sunlight.

You peek around a tree trunk and find you're not alone. Our next heroes are here. A group of forest elephants watches you carefully, trunks raised, sniffing the air. They flap their ears to keep cool, but as soon as you take a step in their direction, they vanish into the forest on the far side of the clearing.

Forest elephants are secretive. They slip away whenever people come near, so they're hard to study. But we know they're the superheroes of the African forest. Their superpowers? An elephant-sized appetite, tough trunk, and formidable feet.

MEET THE CLIMATE HEROES: FOREST ELEPHANTS

If you've seen African elephants at the zoo, they probably weren't forest elephants. Most elephants we see and hear about are savanna elephants. They roam the grassy savannas in search of food and water. Because they're out in the open, they're easy to spot, so we know a lot about them.

Forest elephants, on the other hand, are shy. They're a bit smaller than their grassland cousins and a bit less powerful. But their ecological superpowers are second to none. We know from the evidence they leave behind that they're hard at work as climate heroes.

THE FOREST ELEPHANT!

ELEPHANT-SIZED APPETITE

SECRETIVE AND SHY

TOUGH TRUNK

FORMIDABLE FEET

EXHIBIT A: UPROOTED TREES. Not the massive ones with buttress roots (these climate heroes are big, but not *that* big!). Forest elephants sometimes knock over and uproot little trees—those with trunks no more than a foot across.

EXHIBIT A

The elephants eat more than 500 different kinds of plants, but they're still choosy about the kinds of trees they prefer. They munch on fruits, leaves, bark, even entire branches or trunks of small saplings—whatever they can pluck off a tree or pull from the ground and delicately place in their mouths. They're delicate, but they're also big, so their feeding can get pretty destructive. That can make it obvious when they've traveled through the forest. (That's not always the case. Sometimes their tracks are so hard to follow, it takes all the skills of a forest-dwelling Pygmy tracker to find them.) As strange as it seems, all that eating and apparent destruction help the forest pull more carbon out of the air.

EXHIBIT B: TRAMPLED PATHS. Forest elephants stomp understory plants into the ground when they move through, leaving behind clear trails that crisscross the forest. These are used by all kinds of animals (including leopards, so keep an eye on the branches above you!) and create a kind of highway from one part of the forest to another. They also create clearings like that one you just visited. Forest elephants usually spend time in small groups made up of a female and her young. But they gather in bigger groups in clearings, which might be a place for them to learn from one another, socialize, play, and share critical information about the forest and one another.

EXHIBIT C: MASSIVE PILES OF ELEPHANT POOP. Elephants poop about 17 times a day! That's like going once an hour from the time you wake up until you fall asleep at night. Each pile is chock-full of tree seeds from the fruits the elephants ate deposited in a nice slurry of nutrients. That gives seeds in dung piles an advantage over poop-free seeds. Some will sprout and grow into new trees, which is why some people call forest elephants the gardeners of the forest.

Let's wander along the edge of the clearing and follow one of the trampled paths. Take a close look at the trees near the path. Not the little ones with bent and broken branches, but the big ones farther back. Notice how fat the trunks are. How they tower above

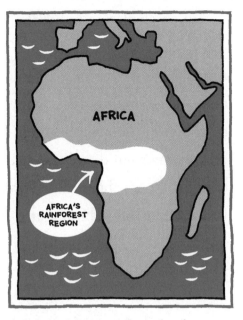

you and everything else in the forest. How their leafy canopies spread wide, shading everything underneath.

These enormous trees are the unsung climate heroes of the African rainforest. But they only grow this big when there are elephants. The same trees in forests without elephants don't grow as tall. Their canopies don't stretch as wide. There are many more trees in elephant-free forests. But even though they have more trees, those forests store less carbon.

How do our elephant heroes make the African forest one of the best climate-protecting places around? By tearing things up.

When elephants move through the forest, they rip up trees, sheer off leaves, and trample seedlings underfoot. But they don't damage or kill old trees. They munch on tasty, fast-growing trees. These preferred plants have lots of protein and sugar in their leaves. Slow-growing trees, on the other hand, are less sweet, tough to chew, and may contain toxic chemicals. Forest elephants thin out the forest, reducing the number of fast-growing trees competing for space. This lets slow-growing trees flourish.

With fewer fast-growing trees trying to grow, there's more water and nutrients for the trees the elephants leave behind. These trees eventually find enough light to allow them to grow into the canopy. A thicker canopy means more shade on the ground, which makes it harder for fast-growing trees to gain a foothold. That means more water and nutrients for the big trees. It's a cycle—around and around we go!

Even though they don't mean to do it, elephants help those slow-growing trees survive and grow to their full height. You can think of it like weeding the forest. Gardeners pull weeds because those unwanted plants take water and nutrients away from the plants the gardeners want to grow. Our climate heroes do the same thing by clearing out the understory.

Removing the competition is part of what elephants do to help the forest, but it's not all. Before you take your next step, you might want to look down. You're about to put your foot in a BIG pile of elephant poop! All kinds of other critters have already discovered it. To one side, a dung beetle pats a bit of poop into place, backs up against its dung ball, and starts rolling it away with its hind feet. The beetle is a climate hero, too. It will bury that dung ball in the forest, and if there are seeds inside, one might just sprout and become a new tree.

You squat down for a closer look at the dung pile and notice it's dotted with seeds. The elephant who left it must have been chowing down on fruit. There are lots of small seeds scattered throughout, but the important seeds for the climate are the big ones. Some are enormous—like flattened tennis balls! A seed this size is stuffed full of food for the seedling that will eventually grow. When it sprouts, the seedling will be bigger and have a better chance of surviving than seedlings coming from smaller seeds.

This big seed came from one of those towering trees. That tree relies on elephants to eat its fruit and poop out seeds in another part of the forest. Moving those seeds far away means new trees won't compete with the parent tree for resources.

Many of the biggest trees in the African rainforest rely on elephants to disperse their seeds in this way. Some tree species have fruits that are only eaten by elephants. Others have fruits that might be eaten by other animals, such as chimpanzees, monkeys, or birds. But even those trees depend partly on elephants because elephants travel the farthest and eat more. The elephants range far and wide across the entire forest, leaving seeds all over the place. It's because of these forest elephant gardeners that you find big trees scattered throughout the forest.

And it's not just depositing the seeds in new places that helps plant trees. Big seeds often have tough coverings. That protects them from animals that nosh on the seeds themselves. Lots of rodents have a hankering for the nutritious insides of a seed. Trees use those tough outer coverings to make it harder for rodents to sniff out the seed. And if they do find it, they have to work harder to reach the softer insides.

The problem? The tough covering makes it harder for the seed to sprout. The seedling only starts to grow when water seeps inside the seed coat. That outer covering blocks water from getting in. But our elephant heroes come to the rescue.

When they chew fruit and swallow it, the seeds get roughed up. Teeth might scrape here and there. But even if it's swallowed without a single tooth mark, the seed is still in for quite a ride. After the elephant swallows, stomach acid goes to work, weakening the seed's outer coat. When that seed is pooped out a day—or two or three—later in another part of the forest, the seed cover isn't so tough anymore. It's weak enough for water to get in, triggering the growth of a brand-new tree. And that helps renew the forest, ensuring our unsung heroes keep going strong.

MEET THE TREES!

Just like phytoplankton and kelp, the unsung heroes of the African rainforest work their magic using photosynthesis. But unlike tiny plankton and even giant kelp, these slow-growing trees get to be massive. And that's the key to their role in protecting the climate.

Some trees grow quickly. These are the ones you tend to find growing in clearings, where there's a lot of sunlight. Others sprout in the shade. These trees grow slower. They take their time building new leaves and branches and adding growth rings to their trunks.

It might seem like growing fast would be good for the climate. The quicker those trees can pull carbon dioxide out of the air, the better. But when trees grow quickly, they make weaker wood. Strong winds can break branches or knock over entire trees. Once it falls, that wood decays, releasing carbon dioxide back into the air. Even fast-growing trees that live for many years die fairly young. Balsa grows super fast—and dies after just 40 years. The average tree lives about 240 years, but some can live for thousands!

Slow and steady has some advantages. Slow-growing trees make hard, dense wood that's tough to break. Why is it so tough? It contains more carbon than the wood of fast-growing trees. If you were to weigh a cubic inch (or cubic centimeter) of wood from one of these trees, it would be heavier than the same amount of wood from a fast-growing tree. The bigger the tree, the more wood it adds each year. As these slow-growing trees eventually stretch high into the forest canopy, they begin to spread out. Their branches form an umbrella over shorter trees. Their leaves soak up lots of sunlight, powering more photosynthesis, allowing the tree to take up more and more carbon dioxide. They store that carbon in their woody tissues and just keep growing.

THE TREES!

FASTER-GROWING TREES IN SUNLIGHT STORE LESS CO_2

SLOWER-GROWING TREES IN THE CANOPY'S SHADE STORE MORE CO_2

HELPING OUR HEROES

Forest elephants are struggling. They're hunted for their ivory tusks and people are taking over their forest home. But you can help! Even if you don't live in Africa, you can donate money to organizations working to protect these important climate heroes. See the Support Our Animal Heroes section at the end of this book for suggestions. You may not have elephants near where you live, but you can still work to protect trees. Plant new ones whenever you can. But even more important: Protect the old, slow-growing trees. Since big trees store more carbon—and remove it from the atmosphere faster—they're a critical part of our fight against climate change. Work with your neighbors to keep trees healthy. Part of this is protecting them from being cut down. But just as important is reducing their exposure to harmful chemicals. Yep, we're back to lawn care.

When people spray their lawns and gardens for weeds, those weed-killing chemicals don't stay put. Some of it does, but often the chemicals drift in the air. Tiny droplets land on trees. Ever see a tree with leaves that are cupped instead of flat? Or maybe they look small, twisted, or kind of wrinkly. These are signs of herbicide damage, and trees are suffering from it everywhere these chemicals are used. With enough exposure, branches or entire trunks may die.

Even if they don't, those small, malformed leaves don't supply as much energy to the tree as healthy leaves would. All this makes trees more sensitive to other stressors, like lack of water or damage from insects that normally wouldn't harm it.

If you haven't had that talk with the adults in your life about their lawn-care practices, it's time. See the Be a Hero at Home section at the end of this book for some resources to help you make your case.

BURYING CLIMATE CHANGE WITH MIGHTY CLAWS!

What has a pouch, lays eggs, and curls up into a spiky ball? One of the smallest climate heroes around!

We're making another big jump, this time to the semiarid forests of Australia. Unlike the tropical rainforests of Africa, it's dry here. There's not much undergrowth to trip you up. Trees are spaced out, leaving plenty of room to move around. Their trunks stretch above your head before splaying into an open canopy of small, tough leaves. They rustle as a gentle breeze causes dappled sunlight to shimmy across the ground. You take a deep breath and find it smells musty, even a bit like cough drops.

In search of our next hero, you wander over the dry, rocky surface. Here and there, you spot pits in the ground: cone-shaped spots where an animal has been digging. Loose soil lies scattered in heaps where it was flung from a recently dug pit.

A raucous laugh up in the canopy makes you stop in your tracks. You glance up to see a brown-and-white kookaburra calling. You're so focused on the bird, you don't watch your step and stumble into a leaf-filled depression. You pull your foot out and find your shoe is covered with decaying leaves and crawling with itty-bitty critters. You give it a good stomp to clean it off and take a closer look.

This pit, created over a year ago, holds the secret to our next hero's climate-fighting abilities. It was created when a short-beaked echidna (ee-KID-nuh) searched for its dinner. Echidnas, also called spiny anteaters, are curious creatures. They nose their way around the soils of Australia in search of ants, termites, and other tasty underground treats. It's their digging that makes them climate heroes here. The pits they leave behind bring together leaf litter, water, and tiny microbes. This combination nourishes trees, shrubs, and other unsung plant heroes. And it buries carbon in the ground.

What happens to leaves when they drop to the ground? They collect as leaf litter. That big pile of leaves you jumped into last fall: leaf litter. It's easy to bag up those fallen leaves and put them out at the curb and forget about them. But they're chock-full of nutritious goodness for all kinds of plants! In places where there's a lot of moisture, those leaves break down and become part of the soil.

Problem is, in much of Australia it's so dry, fallen leaves don't break down. At least, not as part of the soil. They blow about, piling in drifts. Animals trample them, breaking large pieces into smaller ones. When those pieces are exposed to sunlight, they break down even more. But they're not adding carbon to the ground. Instead, sunlight releases carbon dioxide right back into the atmosphere.

We don't want it there! Our echidna heroes help stop this trend by directing leaf carbon into the ground. And they do it with a helping hand from tiny, soil-dwelling sidekicks.

MEET THE CLIMATE HEROES:
ECHIDNAS

The echidna, or spiny anteater, is one of the strangest climate heroes on the planet. Along with its cousin, the platypus, it's the only remaining member of an ancient group of mammals that—get this—lays eggs!

Echidnas also have a pouch, like kangaroos and koalas. A female echidna curls up and deposits a single leathery egg inside her pouch. The egg incubates for about 10 days before a jelly-bean-sized puggle hatches. Like all mammals, echidna moms feed their babies milk. The puggle laps this up while inside the pouch until it grows big (and spiny) enough to safely move around on its own.

THE ECHIDNA!

PROTECTIVE SPINES

SNOUT WITH LONG STICKY TONGUE

BACKWARD-FACING FEET

TERMITES

CLAWS FOR DIGGING

POUCH FOR YOUNG

Echidnas don't have super-speed—at least not when they're walking. In fact, their legs stick out to the side, kind of like a lizard's. They lumber about, clambering over fallen logs and digging in the dirt in search of juicy ants, termites, and beetle larvae. But once they find food, they're super-slurpers: An echidna eats up to 40,000 individual ants and termites each day!

Their secret weapons: a long, narrow snout equipped with an excellent sense of smell and the ability to sense electrical fields given off by grubs. They poke their snouts into the ground in search of food, leaving small depressions in their wake. When they find a tasty treat, they slurp up their prey with a long, sticky tongue. Echidnas don't have teeth, but that's no problem! They use rough pads on the tongue to mash food against the roof of the mouth before swallowing.

Five curved claws on each of their front feet allow them to tear into ant nests or termite mounds with ease. Backward-facing hind feet push loose soil up and out of the pit as they dig. Echidnas are such good diggers, they can bury themselves almost completely in just 60 seconds. Why would they do such a thing? They don't stand a chance of outrunning a predator, but they've got a suit of armor, thanks to the spines that cover them from neck to tail. When threatened, they either curl into a spiky ball or dig down until only their spiny rear ends are poking out of the ground. Predators can't get to the soft underbelly and go off in search of an easier meal.

About the size of a house cat, short-beaked echidnas are common across Australia. They don't have beaks like a bird's or turtle's. The "beak" refers to their long snouts. Short-beaked echidnas have shorter snouts than long-beaked echidnas, which are found only in New Guinea. Short-beaked echidnas live in all kinds of habitats, from semiarid forests and grasslands to wetter regions near the coast. Everywhere they go, they leave pits behind—places where leaf litter and water restore nutrients to tree roots and lock carbon underground.

MEET THE SIDEKICK:
MICROBES

Eucalyptus trees and other kinds of trees and shrubs are definitely the unsung heroes in this system. But we also need to sing the praises of another unseen group: microbes! (Microbe is a general term for organisms too small to be seen without a microscope.) And some slightly larger critters, too.

These tiny organisms play a mighty role in breaking down leaf litter and other dead things. It's easy to think they're gross. After all, what we commonly call "germs" and "creepy-crawlies" aren't exactly what most people think of as heroes. But without them, carbon from dead leaves moves up into the atmosphere instead of down into the ground, where we want it.

Who are these mighty sidekicks?

ARTHROPODS—This is a BIG group of animals, but we're focused on smaller, soil-dwelling ones here. Arthropods have segmented bodies and jointed legs. They include insects, spiders, scorpions, centipedes, even shrimp and lobsters. You won't find any seafood in an echidna pit, but you will find termites, super-small (and super-springy) springtails, and other itty-bitty critters. They eat decaying leaves, helping turn leaf litter into nutrient-rich fertilizer.

BACTERIA—This sounds like a bad thing. After all, some kinds of bacteria can make you sick. But the vast majority of bacteria in the world (and in your body!) are beneficial. These are the good guys—they play an essential role in breaking down dead plants and animals. That releases carbon into the soil, where it can be trapped or taken up by trees.

FUNGI—Fungi are some of the most important decomposers around. They need a fair amount of water to thrive. In semiarid forests, that means we only find them underground or in pits and other places where rainwater collects. Some fungi link tree roots to water and nutrients deep down, too deep for the roots to reach on their own.

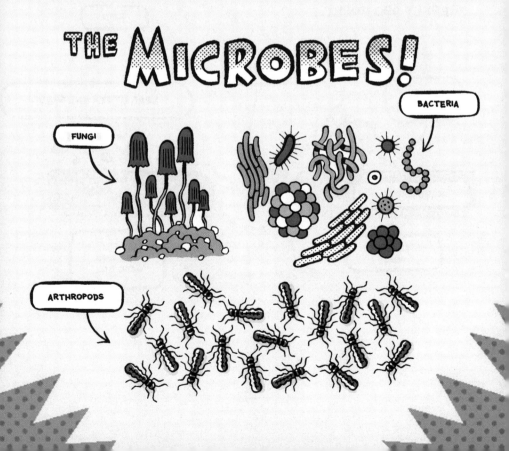

THE MICROBES!

BACTERIA

FUNGI

ARTHROPODS

When an echidna waddles away from a meal, it leaves a pit in the ground. That's a big deal in these dry environments. Rain doesn't fall often, but when it does, it can't soak through the hard-packed earth. Instead, the runoff rushes over the ground, picking up pieces of debris as it goes. Fallen leaves, seeds, bits of bark, fungal spores, and animal poop all get washed along the surface. Water flows downhill, giving the forest floor a good cleaning in the process.

But when echidnas have been busy in the area, some of

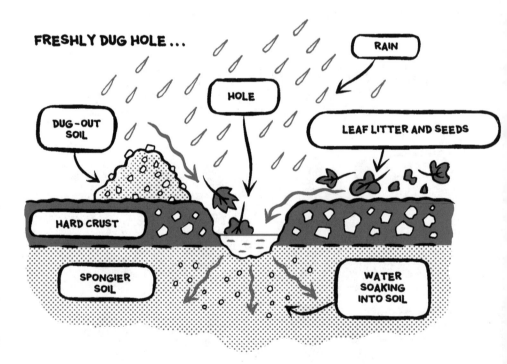

that water takes a different path. It runs into mounds of dirt tossed aside by our diggers. They change the water's flow. Since the dirt wasn't flung far from the pit, some of that water cascades right into the opening.

When our climate hero made the pit, it broke the hard crust of the surface wide open, exposing spongier soil underneath. Runoff flows into the pit and drains into the earth here, soaking belowground where it can provide life-giving water to trees and other plants.

18 MONTHS LATER...

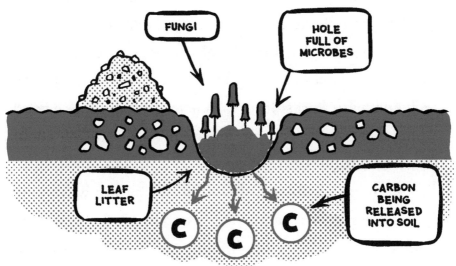

But that's not all. When water fills the pit, it carries all the debris with it. There, leaf litter, seeds, and poop are protected from wind. The deeper the pit, the more debris collects and the harder it is for wind to blow it about. It's protected from sunlight and the drying effects of wind. The temperature stays cooler. Although much of the water soaks in, what's left doesn't evaporate, leaving the contents of the pit damp enough for our miniheroes to get to work.

First come the tiny insects and other creepy-crawlies. They snack on the leaf litter, churning out ever-smaller pieces that can be attacked by bacteria and fungi. The microbes start devouring the plant pieces and poop, breaking them down, returning nutrients, like carbon, back to the soil.

Breaking down leaf litter is a s-l-o-w process in places where it's dry. (When there's plenty of rain, it happens in a matter of weeks.) It can take up to 18 months for an echidna pit to start storing carbon in the soil. So it's a good thing there are lots of our climate heroes waddling about the Australian continent!

But breaking down leaf litter is only part of what these pits are doing. What about those seeds that went bouncing along with the last rainfall? They landed in a spot with good moisture and the beginnings of some good fertilizer. The pit is the perfect spot to germinate—as long as the seed stays put.

All kinds of animals, from ants to birds to mammals, eat seeds. In Australia, ants are the big seed eaters. They roam the forest in search of seeds they can carry back to their nests. But the shape of pits makes it hard for ants to gather the seeds inside of them. Pits have steep sides. Although ants are acrobatic and can cling to all kinds of surfaces, they can't easily carry a big seed up a cliff. So most seeds stay safe in the pits, where they can grow into new plants.

MUCH LATER...

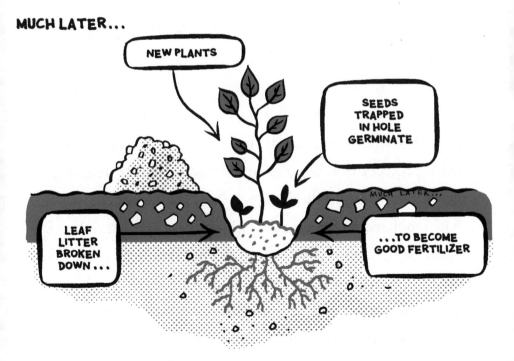

Older echidna pits are great places for new trees and shrubs to grow. These plants add to the forest over time. And just like we've seen with our other unsung heroes, their growth uses carbon, which is then locked away inside the plants. We hope it will stay there for a long, long time.

HELPING OUR HEROES

What can you do to help out our heroes? If you're in Australia, support efforts to protect digging mammals. Although echidnas are doing well across the continent, other digging animals, such as bettongs and bilbies, are not. These creatures also leave pits behind—some much deeper than echidna pits. They create the ideal spot to trap carbon and fight climate change.

Don't live in Australia? There are things you can do, no matter where you live. Find out what kinds of digging animals live in your part of the world—and what you can do to protect them. Diggers are often called ecosystem engineers. They completely change the way the ecosystem works when they search for a meal. Without these animals to break up the soil, rain may not soak into the earth. Seeds may not germinate. Trees might wither and die. Even though they seem destructive, diggers are essential to their ecosystems.

Free-roaming cats pose a big threat to these climate heroes. They might be feral cats—animals that live in the wild. Or they might be pets that people allow outside. Cats are cunning hunters, killing billions of animals every year. No matter where you live, you can help our climate heroes by keeping cats indoors. (See the Additional Information section at the back of this book for more information about free-roaming cats.)

You can also play the role of a digger right at home. If your family doesn't compost, you should try it. When fall comes, don't bag up those leaves. Instead, move them off the lawn and onto mulched areas. Leaves make great mulch. Or build a compost bin and put the leaves there.

Add some grass clippings and kitchen scraps. Mix it now and then, water if it doesn't rain much, and watch all those leftovers turn into a fine compost that you can spread on your garden—or over your lawn, now that it's not being fertilized anymore.

Some people compost by digging holes next to their flowers and burying their kitchen scraps. These break down faster than the stuff thrown into a compost bin, providing all kinds of nutrients to the plants. Bonus: no more stinky garbage cans!

You can do one more thing: Be careful not to start any wildfires. Although many forest fires start from lightning strikes, many more begin when someone builds a fire when they shouldn't—or even creates a spark near dry plants. If you explore the wilderness, be sure to follow rules about when and where you can start a fire. And be sure to put your fire out completely before leaving the area. All it takes is a single ember riding on a gust of wind to burn down an entire forest, releasing all that stored carbon right back into the atmosphere.

FIGHTING CLIMATE CHANGE
WITH **EVERY MOVE!**

We hear a lot about carbon and climate change, but we don't always hear as much about our climate heroes or the ecosystems in which they live. Natural systems provide us with important services. They clean water, remove pollution, and move carbon from one place to another. Sometimes carbon moves out of the air and into plants, animals, and the oceans. Sometimes it moves in the other direction.

Climate is complicated. But one thing is simple: We need our climate heroes to help us in this fight.

And not only the ones described in this book! There are many more out there, doing what they do, working with the unsung heroes of the world to put carbon where it can't heat the planet. But many of these animals, plants, and ecosystems are in trouble. In order to fight climate change, we must protect our climate heroes. That's true of all natural systems around the world. They sustain us, but only if we sustain them.

That means *you* are an essential climate hero, too.

MEET THE CLIMATE HERO: YOU!

Take a good look in the mirror. Check out your height. The color of your hair, skin, and eyes. Whether you have a snaggle tooth. Whatever you see, that's what a climate hero looks like. Because no matter who you are, *you* have the power to help fight climate change.

Being a climate hero is all about actions. They don't have to be big actions, either. They can be as small as turning off the lights when you leave a room, persuading your parents to buy an electric car, or riding your bike instead of driving.

Climate change feels like an enormous problem. It *is* an enormous problem. When you're just one person, it doesn't always feel like you can do anything about it, but you can. Every small change makes an impact. There are 8 billion people on the planet. If everyone took the same small steps they would add up in a hurry.

Once you've mastered the small stuff, think bigger. You may be a student, but your words have power. Don't believe it? Check out Greta Thunberg, who went from being the only person at the first School Strike for Climate to meeting with world leaders to talk about how entire governments need to tackle climate change. She wasn't old enough to vote when she did that. Greta's no longer the only young person working to fix the climate crisis. Young people from around the world are making their voices heard so they can

enjoy a future with a calm, predictable climate. All it takes to be a climate hero is a little persistence.

BE A HERO

So how can you be a climate hero? You can start with the suggestions at the end of each chapter. Here are a few more ideas to keep you going:

Plant a flower garden full of native plants to support pollinators and other wildlife. Not only is it beautiful to look at, it doesn't require as much maintenance as a lawn. Native plants are adapted to the local climate. That makes them easier to care for. They also do a better job of supporting wildlife than non-native plants. The critters in your area are adapted to eating native plants, so give them a buffet. You will see some damage to your plants. That's a sign that insects and animals are chowing down at your buffet. Hang tight! It's usually only for a few weeks, and then the plants will recover. After all, you can't have butterflies without feeding the caterpillars.

Plant a vegetable garden. Most of our fresh produce is shipped long distances. A garden provides fresh fruits and vegetables without all that exhaust and pollution. Plus, homegrown food just tastes better.

Buy local. Shipping releases huge amounts of carbon dioxide into the atmosphere. Go to a farmers market or sign up for a Community Supported Agriculture (CSA) program near you. CSAs allow you to pay a local farm to grow food—and you get fresh produce every week.

Symbolically adopt an animal. Instead of getting or giving stuffed animals, consider "adopting" a live one instead. Adopt-an-animal programs support efforts by organizations working to help threatened animals, from sea otters to elephants and everything in between. You won't get to cuddle your adopted animal, but you will be helping to keep it alive and well, so it can continue to be a climate hero. See the Resources section at the end of this book for more information on how to symbolically adopt an animal.

Encourage adults to drive smarter. Maybe a new car isn't in your adults' budget right now. That's okay! Encourage them to turn off the engine instead of letting it idle. It's easy to leave a car running when you're waiting. Maybe they're picking you up from sports practice or sitting in the drive-through. Instead of idling the engine, ask them to turn it off. In addition to climate benefits, it reduces pollution (which is good for you), and saves money on gas (which is good for them). If they're going to idle more than about 10 seconds, they should shut the engine off. (To provide proof, share the link to the Engineering Explained video in the Resources section of this book.)

Take public transportation. This may not be available where you live, but if it is, it's a great way to get around.

Bonus: Your adults don't have to deal with the stress of traffic. And if you're old enough and your parents say it's okay, you can get around by yourself.

Turn off lights and fans. If no one needs them, why leave them on? You may think you're keeping the room cool by leaving the fan running, but fans are only cooling if you're there to feel the breeze. They don't actually change the temperature of the room. Wasting electricity may not seem like it contributes to climate change, but most electricity comes from coal-burning or natural-gas power plants that release carbon dioxide to power your home.

Put computers, TVs, and other electronics on power strips. Turn the strips off when they're not in use or use power strips that do this for you. Many electronics are in a state of suspended animation when they're off, waiting to reactivate, and that takes energy.

Suggest Energy Star appliances. When your household needs to buy new appliances, light bulbs, or a new air conditioner or water heater, tag along on the shopping trip. It may seem boring, but you can have a big impact. Make sure your adults look for Energy Star products. The Energy Star seal tells you the appliance uses less energy than others. Again, less electricity means less carbon dioxide—at least until we make the jump to renewable energy.

Organize or participate in a student climate march. It's not just individual people who need to make changes. We need governments to act, as well. There are lots of opportunities to get involved and make your voice heard.

Educate your adults on what you've learned. Make sure they know it's your future at stake! Ask them to contact their government representatives to encourage action on climate change. Have them take you to a climate rally. Ask to visit a state or national park. Pick up trash when you find it.

Once you get up close and personal with the beauty of our world's natural systems and the climate heroes they protect, everyone will want to do more.

You are a climate hero, too. Suit up! It's time to get to work.

ADDITIONAL INFORMATION

ALGAL BLOOMS

Although algal blooms can do a lot of good for the ocean and reduce climate change, not all algal blooms are beneficial. Some can be downright harmful. In fact, that's what they're called: harmful algal blooms.

Harmful algal blooms happen when an algal bloom contains types of algae that release toxins. These can poison sea life, including fish. Clams and mussels eat the algae and store the toxins in their bodies. When seabirds, marine mammals, or people eat the contaminated shellfish, they can become ill, experience severe disorders, or even die.

When algal blooms happen, the mass of algae eventually dies and sinks. It decays, and the bacteria that break down the algae use up oxygen in the water. This can cause fish and other aquatic animals to suffocate and die, even when the algae aren't toxic.

Scientists are working hard to understand what causes harmful algal blooms, so they can predict when they are likely to happen. Someday they might be able to prevent them, but not yet.

HEALTHY SNACKS

Why mention specific foods when you need to sweet-talk your adults into rethinking lawn care? Fruits and many vegetables (including tomatoes and peppers), nuts, and ice cream all need pollinators. Honey nut cereal? Yep—for the honey AND the nuts. Bees aren't the only pollinators. Ants, flies, bats, and butterflies—even some mosquitoes—also move pollen from flower to flower. Take pollinators away and these foods disappear from our kitchens.

Pollinators and other insects are in serious trouble, in part because of our lawn-care practices. Mowing less often and letting clover, dandelions, violas, and other flowering plants grow provides a buffet for pollinators. Find out other ways to help pollinators at the Xerces Society: https://xerces.org/pollinator-conservation

COMPOSTING

You can help turn leaf litter and kitchen waste into nutrient-rich compost right at home. All you need is a little space for a compost bin. You can buy one—some even have tumblers to make it easier to mix. Or you can build one. It can be big, with multiple bins, or just a pile where you toss yard waste.

The key is to add an even mix of browns (like dead leaves or plain cardboard) and greens (grass clippings and any fruit or vegetable remains, plus coffee or tea). You can also throw in eggshells. Toss in just about any kitchen waste except meat, which won't break down easily and can get stinky pretty quickly.

LEAVE THE LEAVES

It may seem like leaves are a problem. We sure spend a lot of time raking, blowing, and mowing them up. But they're an important part of the ecosystem, recycling all kinds of nutrients back into the soil. And they do more than that: Leaves provide important places for all kinds of animals to spend the winter. Removing leaves harms habitat all around.

The next time your adults ask you to help bag the leaves, suggest moving them off the lawn and onto garden spaces instead. There they can provide that critical habitat. When they break down, they provide more nutrients to plants than wood mulch does. And they're just as good as mulch at protecting plants from hot, cold, and dry weather.

FREE-ROAMING CATS

Free-roaming cats are one of the biggest threats to animals around the world. They kill up to 4 billion birds and up to 22 billion mammals each year—and that's just in the United States! They also go after reptiles and amphibians—pretty much anything they can catch. Cats are some of the best predators around. They're patient and stealthy, which makes it easy for them to sneak up on unsuspecting prey. If cats only hunted to eat, that would be one thing. But they often leave the dead animal behind before searching out a new one. Ever find a "present" from your cat on the porch? It's one of many kills the cat made.

Even if they don't succeed in catching animals, cats can make it harder for native animals to safely find food or

raise young. Over time, populations of these essential native critters shrink. Invasive animals, like house mice, take their place.

Outdoor cats are also more likely to be injured or killed by cars, people, or other wildlife. To show that you care for your cat (and the environment), keep it inside!

RESOURCES TO HELP OUR CLIMATE HEROES

SUPPORT OUR ANIMAL HEROES

You can symbolically adopt an animal to help support efforts to protect its species in the wild. Check out the World Wildlife Fund's Symbolic Species Adoptions. This program lets you protect all kinds of climate heroes, from whales to sea otters to elephants: gifts.worldwildlife.org/gift-center/gifts/Species-Adoptions.aspx

Thanks to their spines, echidnas are doing well in Australia, but other digging mammals are not. You can support the return of bilbies, bettongs, and other native mammals to habitats from which they've disappeared by donating to Arid Recovery: aridrecovery.org.au

BE A HERO AT HOME

These resources can help you have important talks with the adults in your life. This is just a start—there are many more resources out there. Do additional research if you need more info!

Many adults have been told that car engines use more gas to start than to idle, but that's not true anymore. Show this to any adults you know who hesitate to turn off the engine:

Explained, Engineering. 2018. "Americans Have No Idea How Much Fuel Idling Uses." YouTube. September 5, 2018. https://www.youtube.com/watch?v=dFImHhNwbJo.

Cubie, Doreen. 2019. "A Farewell to Lawns." National Wildlife Federation. April 1, 2019. https://nwf.org/Mag azines/National-Wildlife/2019/April-May/Gardening/ Turf-Lawns.

Mackenzie, Jillian. 2019. "How to Combat Weeds . . . Gently." Natural Resources Defense Council. June 25, 2019. https://www.nrdc.org/stories/how-combat-weeds-gently.

n.d. Beyond Pesticides. https://www.beyondpesticides. org/.

ADDITIONAL READING

Giannella, Valentina, and Manuela Marazzi. 2019. *We Are All Greta: Be Inspired to Save the World*. London: Laurence King Publishing.

Jackson, Tom and Dragan Kordić. 2021. *How do we stop climate change?* Weldon Owen.

Joyner, Andrew. 2020. *Stand Up! Speak Up!: A Story Inspired by the Climate Change Revolution*. New York: Schwartz & Wade Books.

Kirby, Loll and Adelina Lirius. 2020. *Old Enough to Save the Planet*. New York: Magic Cat Publishing.

McAnulty, Stacy. 2022. *Save the People! Halting Human Extinction*. New York: Little, Brown and Company.

Sicwalt, Dany and Aurélia Durand. 2022. *This Book Will Save the Planet*. London: Frances Lincoln Children's Books.

ACKNOWLEDGMENTS

I am grateful to the huge number of people who are actively working to protect both our climate and our natural systems. I hope this book helps raise awareness of just how vital—and intertwined—their efforts are.

Thanks to Laura Godwin, Kortney Nash, and the team at Godwin Books/Henry Holt. I'm thrilled to be doing another book with you! Thanks to Bonnie Cutler, Maria Vlasak, and Kristen Stedman for their excellent copy edits. Thanks to Jennifer Keenan and Mallory Grigg for doing an awesome job designing this book and to Jie Yang for being a diligent production manager. And thank you to Jason for for his fabulous illustrations.

All the information included in this book exists thanks to the hard work of many scientists. Thank you for sharing your work with the world! I would especially like to thank Joe Roman, Stephen Blake, Joshua Smith, and David Eldridge for reading sections of the manuscript to vet it for accuracy. Any remaining errors are my own.

Nancy Sharp Wagner, Jenny Heithoff, and Emily Timm, thanks for reading an early draft of this book; your feedback is invaluable. Alex Weiss, thanks for your feedback and support—you're the best!

Cole and Lane, I know I share a lot of random information from my research at the dinner table; thanks for listening and for the engaging discussions that follow. Jeff, you make this writing gig possible. I'm so grateful to be able to do something I love with the full support of my family.